Layers

WALLS, Volume 1

ECHO SHADE

Published by TJ TSELE, 2024.

While every precaution has been taken in the preparation of this book, the publisher assumes no responsibility for errors or omissions, or for damages resulting from the use of the information contained herein.

LAYERS

First edition. July 31, 2024.

ISBN: 979-8227140128

Written by ECHO SHADE.

Table of Contents

To the wanderers of worlds and the dreamers of the deep, this collection is for you. May these poems be your companions on journeys both within and beyond, lighting up paths yet untraveled. In every word, find a friend; in every verse, a home. Thank you for allowing my thoughts to dance in the quiet corners of your minds. This e-book is not just my creation, it is a tapestry woven from the threads of our shared human experience. Enjoy the adventure.

"LAYERS" is an evocative journey through the myriad shades of love, a poetry collection that delves deep into the heart's labyrinth. Each poem is a heartbeat, pulsating with the raw emotions of love found, love lost, and love's rebirth. From the dizzying heights of seduction to the abyss of heartbreak, this book captures the insanity of love's grip and the tranquil wisdom found in healing. The verses weave a tapestry of passion, exploring love's intricate complexities with a tender touch that both burns and soothes. This anthology is not just a book; it's a companion for the soul, a mirror reflecting the universal truths of love's eternal dance. Embrace the beauty, endure the pain, and emerge transformed with "LAYERS."

Hearsay in Love

In the realm of whispered winds and silent hues,
A soul wanders, untouched by love's deep blues.
Hearsay's their guide through love's vast domain,
Where secrets bloom like flowers after rain.
"He said, she said," the common chorus sings,
Of love's sweet highs and heartache's piercing stings.
Yet, to this heart, it's but a distant tale,
A mythic quest for Holy Grail so frail.
Rumors of love, like shadows in the night,
Cast shapes on walls, just out of plain sight.
A secret dance of silhouettes unknown,
To this lone heart, love's truth remains unshown.
Whispers of passion, rumors of a kiss,
Are but echoes of a chance they might miss.
For love, to them, is a sealed treasure chest,
Heard of in stories, where fantasies rest.
In every rumor, a sliver of doubt,
In every secret, wonder wanders about.
Is love the sun, a truth that always gleams?
Or the moon's phase, a cycle of dreams?
They ponder deep, this heart so unacquainted,
With love's true face, so often painted.
A canvas of hearsay, not of firsthand art,
Leaves them guessing, piecing love's chart.
So here they stand, at the edge of affection's lore,
Curious of the feelings they've not felt before.
Love—a concept wrapped in whispers and peeks,

ECHO SHADE

A puzzle to solve, a language one seeks.
Mayhap one day, this heart will find its part,
In love's grand play, and with a genuine start.
Till then, they'll listen to the he said, she said,
And dream of the day love's book is read.

Moral Compass of Love

In the name of love, would you traverse the darkest seas?
Would you challenge the fiercest storms, bend your noblest knees?
In the name of love, would you question the stars above,
Ponder right from wrong, in the pursuit of love?
Would you cross the line that divides the just from sin,
In the name of love, where does your loyalty begin?
Would you hold it close, a flame against the night,
Or let it slip away, a bird taking flight?
In the name of love, would you face the deepest fears,
Confront the hidden truths, and shed the hardest tears?
Would you break the chains of morality's tight grasp,
In the name of love, would you dare to ask?
For love is a force that knows no bounds,
It speaks in actions, in whispers, in sounds.
It can build a bridge where none did exist,
In the name of love, would you take that risk?
Would you stand alone against a tide of doubt,
In the name of love, is that what it's about?
Would you give it all, leave nothing behind?
In the name of love, what would you find?
Would you search your soul, where the shadows dwell?
In the name of love, would you break the spell?
Would you rise above, where the eagles soar?
In the name of love, could you ask for more?
For love is a quest, a journey, a fight,
It's a beacon in darkness, a flicker of light.
It's a four-letter word, so simple, so clear,

ECHO SHADE

In the name of love, would you draw it nearby?
Would you brave the storm, would you endure the test?
In the name of love, would you give your best?
Would you walk the path, though it's paved with pain?
In the name of love, what would you gain?
For love is a gamble, a leap in the dark,
It's a vow, a whisper, a hopeful spark.
It's a question asked, with a trembling heart,
In the name of love, would you play that part?
Would you risk it all, not knowing the cost,
In the name of love, could it all be lost?
Would you step into the void, without a safety net,
In the name of love, how far would you get?
For love is a power, fierce and wild,
It's tender as a flower, free as a child.
It's a dance, a dream, a promise made,
In the name of love, would you be afraid?
Would you push the limits, would you bend the rules?
In the name of love, are there any fools?
Would you give your all, would you go that far?
In the name of love, that's what you are.

Sailor's Heart: Between Devil and Sea

In love's treacherous waters, we sail,
Between passion's fire and the abyss's wail.
The devil whispers sweet nothings of desire,
While the deep blue sea hums a siren's choir.
To choose the devil is to dance with flame,
A fervent tango, a perilous game.
Yet, to choose the sea, so vast and profound,
Is to drift in depths where one might drown.
In the arms of love, we're sailors lost,
Navigating hearts, whatever the cost.
The devil's embrace, a fiery cage,
The sea's caress, an endless stage.
Love, the captain, steers us through,
Between the devil and the deep blue hue.
A dilemma as old as time's own thread,
Where hearts are won, and tears are shed.
For in the devil's eyes, we see our fears,
In the sea's song, our hopes and tears.
Each choice a gamble, a fate untold,
In love's domain, where stories unfold.
So here we stand, in love's grand scheme,
Between a devil's deal and a sea-bound dream.
A metaphor for the lover's plight,
In the dance of day and the still of night.
The devil offers a fiery touch,
A promise of much, yet not enough.
The sea, a mystery, deep and wide,

ECHO SHADE

In its blue embrace, we long to hide.
Between these two, our hearts are torn,
In the space where love and doubt are born.
A dilemma faced by all who yearn,
For a love that's true, for which we burn.
So let us ponder this age-old scene,
Of devils red and seas of green.
For in the end, it's love we seek,
In its strength, we find, in its weakness, we're meek.
May we navigate with care and grace,
Between the devil's grin and the sea's embrace.
For love is a journey, not a destination,
A series of choices, a lifelong equation.
And though we may falter, may we always find,
A way through the dilemmas that love entwined.
For between the devil and the deep blue sea,
Lies the heart's voyage, wild and free.

Silhouettes in Sync

In the grand ballroom of love, where hearts sway,
Two souls step forth, in a dance to portray.
A tender beginning, soft music, a glance,
The art of romance, mirrored in dance.
With hands gently clasped, they begin to move,
Each step a statement, as they find their groove.
A twirl like a promise, a dip like a trust,
In this ballroom, love's rhythm is a must.
The lead and follow, a delicate art,
Reflects how in love, we each play a part.
A step forward, a step back, in harmony,
Like lovers who navigate life's symphony.
The dance floor's embrace, where secrets are told,
Is akin to love's journey, both new and old.
A leap of faith here, a careful sidestep,
In dance as in love, it's the pattern we prep.
For in every performance, there's risk and thrill,
As in love, where we climb each emotional hill.
A spin may falter, a step may be missed,
But in the arms of love, such flaws are kissed.
The music crescendos, a passionate rise,
Like the fervor of love in a lover's eyes.
A swift paso doble or a waltz's grace,
Each movement a chapter in love's embrace.
And when the music inevitably slows,
As in love, where sometimes a quiet wind blows,
They hold each other close, savor the beat,

ECHO SHADE

In ballroom or love, such moments are sweet.
For the parallels of dance and love are clear,
In steps and in heartbeats, we hold dear.
Through each routine and every loving day,
We dance, we love, in life's grand ballet.

Eternal Acolyte

In the cathedral of my heart, a silent prayer ascends,
For a love that's divine, where the sacred never ends.
You, a deity in flesh, an idol carved so fine,
I worship at your altar, where love and faith entwine.
Your whispers are the hymns that in the darkness shine,
Each word a sacred scripture, a testament divine.
In the gospel of your gaze, I find my holy writ,
With every look, you bless me, in devotion, I submit.
Your touch, a benediction, grace upon my skin,
A fervent disciple, I revel in this sin.
The sacrament of your kiss, a chalice of sweet wine,
I drink in your essence, inebriated by the divine.
In the doctrine of your love, I've found my hallowed creed,
For you are the messiah of my soul's deepest need.
A pilgrim in your love, I journey without end,
Seeking salvation in your arms, where broken hearts mend.
Your love, the steeple that pierces through my night,
Guiding me like a beacon, with its celestial light.
In the scripture of your presence, I've found my sacred text,
A canon of devotion, upon which my faith is wreathed.
In the liturgy of our love, I find my sanctified place,
A temple of fervor, built within your embrace.
You are the religion that sets my spirit free,
In the church of your passion, I find my sanctuary.
So let me be the acolyte, who serves you with each breath,
In the religion of your love, I'll be devout till death.
For in the creed of your affection, I've found my holy grail,

ECHO SHADE

In the worship of your essence, my devotion will not fail.
In this faith of fervent ardor, I am hopelessly ensnared,
A disciple of your love eternally declared.
For you are the divinity, in human form revealed,
In the sanctity of loving you, my fate is forever sealed.

Gallery of My Mind

In the quiet solitude of my mind's gentle embrace,
I craft a world where distance cannot intrude,
Where your visage, so vivid, stands before me with grace,
And our hearts converse in silent interlude.
I paint you in the hues of my deepest desires,
In scenarios spun from the threads of yearning,
Each thought a brushstroke, each dream that aspires,
To a closeness that my soul keeps on turning.
In the gallery of my mind, you're a masterpiece of thought,
A creation born from the longing in my chest,
With every imagined touch, my breath is caught,
In the fantasy of us, I find my rest.
I see us dancing beneath the moon's soft glow,
In a world where the stars align just right,
Where the whispers of the wind come slow,
And the universe fades behind your light.
In the quiet café on the corner of my dreams,
We share laughter over cups of imagined tea,
The warmth in your eyes, a gentle stream,
Of love that flows, though you're not here with me.
Through fields of gold, we run without a care,
In a daydream where I can call you mine,
With every step, I shake off my despair,
For in these moments, our lives intertwine.
I've built a bridge across the chasm of space,
With pillars of hope and cables of trust,
Though I know not the contours of your face,

ECHO SHADE

In my mind, you're more than just a wistful gust.
You're the lighthouse in the fog of my reality,
A beacon that guides my heart's ship through,
Though you're a world away, in my fantasy,
I'm right there, admiring, loving you.

Think Of Me

In the hush of night's embrace,
Where whispers trace the heart's deep space,
A yearning stirs, so bittersweet,
For the one you cannot meet.
A shadow's touch, a silent plea,
For them to think of you, to see
The echo of a love not had,
The wanting drives you near to mad.
In dreams, they come, so close, so far,
A forbidden dance, a distant star.
You crave their thought, their slightest glance,
In someone else's arms, perchance.
To want what's just beyond your reach,
A lesson that the stars do teach.
A burning, yearning, deep desire,
To be the focus of their fire.
A name whispered in the dark,
Leaves upon your soul a mark.
A ghostly touch, a fleeting look,
An unwritten, boundless book.
In the theater of your mind,
You dance with shadows, love unkind.
The art of longing, sweet seduction,
In every word, a new construction.
You linger in the realm of 'almost',
Where feelings are a haunting ghost.
The idea of them fills your night,

ECHO SHADE

Their absence a relentless plight.
A craving that defies all reason,
A longing through each passing season.
A silent wish for them to feel,
Your presence, a desire to steal.
For in this dance of silent yearning,
It's not the end for which you're burning.
But the chase, the dream, the constant state,
Of wanting what the fates berate.
So let this poem be the voice,
Of your heart's clandestine choice.
To desire, to want, to yearn, to dream,
In love's complex, eternal scheme.

Hold Me

Envelop me within your arms, as though I'm precious art,
Embrace me tight, so I won't ever feel we'll part.
Cradle me as if I'm the keeper of your heart's chart,
Cherish me as though from the very start, we're not apart.
Shield me in the tempest, be my sturdy weather chart,
Caress me gently, like a feather's lightest part.
Absorb my tears, as a sponge takes water in its part,
Comfort me, like childhood toys that never depart.
Be the balm that soothes the aches that in my heart doth dart,
Hold me, for without me, your world might fall apart.
Let my nearness wash away the sins that on you tart,
Prefer a loss in battle, than from my love to depart.
Wrap me in the solace of your love's endless mart,
Hold me with a promise that we'll never be apart.
Hold me with the truth that in your life, I'm a vital part,
Hold me as the masterpiece of your life's art.
Hold me with a passion that burns bright, a fiery dart,
Hold me as the symphony in your life's concert part.
Hold me as the anchor that in your sea won't depart,
Hold me as the harmony to your soul's counterpart.
Hold me as the light that guides you through the dark,
Hold me as the signature that marks your life's remark.
Hold me as the vow that time will never outsmart.
Embrace me in your warmth as though I'm delicate lace,
Cherish me tenderly, in your love's gentle embrace.
Cradle me close, like the rarest gem ever found,
Treasure me silently, without a single sound.

ECHO SHADE

Shield me with your might from the tempest's roar,
Caress me gently, as waves do kiss the shore.
Absorb my sorrows, as the earth takes the rain,
Comfort me softly and take away the pain.
Cure me with your touch, let it mend all that aches,
Value me dearly, for true love's never fake.
Hold me with a promise that time cannot erase,
Bind me with a bond that distance cannot chase.
Nurture me like a melody that soothes the soul,
Protect me with a fervor that makes me whole.
Enfold me in your dreams, where I can dance and spin,
Keep me in your thoughts, where I've always been.
Guard me like the dawn guards the morning's first light,
Preserve me with a passion that feels just right.
Embrace me with a strength that never knows defeat,
Secure me with a trust that makes one complete.
Sustain me with a hope that in your heart does dwell,
Cherish me, as a story that only we can tell.
Hold me in a moment that lasts an eternity,
Keep me in a love that's bound by destiny.
Hold me with a care that's as deep as the sea,
Hold me, for in your arms is where I'm meant to be.

Senses

It begins with a whisper of touch, a ballet of fingertips dancing across the canvas of skin, tracing contours as delicate as lace. Your lips, a tender conspirator, graze my ear, murmuring sweet nothings that serenade my soul, daring to weave tales of love.

Your hands chart a course, a slow and deliberate expedition to the small of my back, where patience is a virtue and time bends to our will. You map the terrain of my skin, a gentle conquest, as I strive to maintain the facade of calm, my composure a fragile fortress under your tender siege.

The proximity of you ignites a warmth, a radiant heat that envelops me, sending my senses into a whirlwind, dizzy with desire. I find solace in the solidity of a chair, grounding myself in the midst of this sensory storm.

And when distance dares to divide, your scent remains, a ghostly presence, an aromatic echo that fills the void, a lingering reminder of the intimacy we shared, a sensory sonnet composed in the language of touch, taste, scent, sound, and sight.

In the symphony of our encounter, taste and sound play the maestros of our senses. The taste, a fusion of flavors, where your kiss is a delicacy, a confectionery of passion that dissolves on the tongue, sweet, with hints of longing. It's an intimate feast, where every morsel is a word unspoken, every sip a promise kept. The sound, a harmony of whispers and heartbeats, a crescendo of soft sighs and muted moans that compose the melody of our connection. Your laughter is a chime, a sound that resonates with the rhythm of joy, while the cadence of your voice in the quietude of night is a lullaby that lulls my senses into a tranquil reverie.

Together, taste and sound interlace to narrate our story, a sensory ballad that echoes through the chambers of memory, long after our parting. It's a narrative written not in ink, but in the flavors savored on the lips and the resonances that linger in the ear, a testament to the moments shared and cherished.

L. S. D.

In the shadowed corners of a love that burns too bright, there lies a tale of passion that mirrors the perilous dance with the forbidden. You, my elixir, my sweetest downfall, with every encounter, we chase the fleeting high. More than a mere six times, we indulge, and oh, how divine it feels.

You are the smoke that curls around my being, and I, the breath that draws you in. Together, we awaken, enlightened by the substances that bind us. We are intoxicated by the very essence of each other, lost in a haze of euphoria.

I belong to you, and you to me, in a world where only we exist. We drown in the heady wine of our love, letting it pour over us, consuming us. In this intoxication, we find our truth, our reason, our everything.

You are the drug that courses through my veins, and I, the pill that promises paradise. We savor the connection, the plug that fills the void, knowing well the price it demands. Yet, we are willing to pay, for what is life without this sweet poison?

You are my one and only, the flame that ignites my soul. I am your burning desire, the fire that never dies. Look at the blaze we have created, a conflagration born of our union. Together, we have ignited a fire that could either warm us or consume us whole.

In the quiet aftermath, where the embers of our fiery passion slowly fade to ash, we find ourselves amidst the ruins of a love that once blazed too fiercely. The air is thick with the scent of burnt dreams, and the silence is a stark contrast to the cacophony of our union's zenith. We wander through the desolation, our footsteps echoing in the hollow chambers of our hearts, where the echoes of laughter and whispers of devotion are now just ghosts that haunt us.

The intoxication has worn off, leaving behind a sobering clarity that pierces through the haze of our once-addictive love. We see the scars, the burns that mark our souls, reminders of the price we paid for dancing too close to the flames. The wine that once flowed so freely, fuelling our reckless abandon, has turned to vinegar on our lips, a bitter reminder of what we have lost.

We reach for each other, but the connection that once electrified us now feels like a static shock, a jolt that reminds us that some things, once broken, can never be fully mended. The plug that once filled us, that once made us feel whole, has been pulled, and we are left feeling empty, drained of the very essence that once defined us.

The fire that we made, that we thought would warm us through the coldest nights, has instead scorched the very foundation of our being. We stand amidst the charred remains, wondering if the warmth was ever worth the inevitable destruction. The drug, the pill, the sweet poison that we savored—it has left us with a withdrawal that gnaws at our insides, a craving for a fix that we know we must deny ourselves.

Our love, once a beacon that lit up the night, has dimmed, and we are left in the darkness, trying to find our way back to a light that no longer guides us. The desire that once burned so brightly now flickers weakly, struggling to survive in the cold reality that dawns upon us.

We are survivors of a love that consumed everything in its path, a love that promised us the stars but left us in the void. We are the aftermath, the survivors of our own hearts' reckless decisions. We must now learn to navigate a world that seems less vibrant, less alive, without the intoxicating high of our explosive romance.

The aftermath is a landscape of what-ifs and could-have-beens, a place where the memories of our love are both a sanctuary and a prison. We are haunted by the specters of our past selves, those versions of us that knew no bounds, that flew too close to the sun. Now, with wings singed and spirits heavy, we must find the strength to rebuild, to find a new way to soar.

In the end, the aftermath of our love is a testament to the human spirit's resilience. It is a story of loss, but also of hope—a hope that from the ashes of a love that burned too bright, new growth can emerge, tender and green, reaching towards the light. It is a reminder that even the most explosive of loves can leave behind seeds that, with care and time, can bloom into something just as beautiful, if not more so, in its tranquillity and grace.

Made in China

Within the silent chambers of my heart, where love once brightly shone,
Now lies a gallery of porcelain and glass, cold and forlorn.
Each piece a fragile memory, a testament of care,
A delicate dance of caution, a waltz of despair.
The teacup, with its cracked rim, whispers of gentle lips,
That sipped from its hollow, now silent since our eclipse.
The vase, once home to roses, stands empty, a hollow guard,
Of the thorns left behind, and petals that fell hard.
The mirror, with its shattered face, reflects a soul so torn,
A mosaic of what was, in shards of heartbreak born.
And there, the glass figurine, poised in frozen grace,
A symbol of what I held dear, now lost without a trace.
Handle with care, the signs implore, for love is but brittle ware,
A single slip, a moment's lapse, and cracks appear bare.
So I tread lightly through this fragile trove,
Where once was love, now caution reigns, and memories softly rove.
Amidst the quiet of the night, I hear the echoes clear,
Of laughter once shared, now a chime of fear.
The goblet of our love, once brimming with sweet wine,
Now stands empty, a brittle relic of a bond once divine.
The porcelain doll, with her painted, smiling face,
Mocks the joy we knew, in this now desolate place.
Her glassy eyes, unblinking, hold no comfort, no solace,
A stark reminder of a love that time will never efface.
In the stillness, I cradle a lone, unbroken plate,
A symbol of hope, perhaps it's not too late.
Yet, as I hold it close, I feel the surface mar,

ECHO SHADE

A crack, then a shatter, as it joins the rest, ajar.
So I build a fortress from the fragments of our past,
A barricade of caution, for my heart to hold fast.
But even as I shield it, I know the truth deep within,
That even the strongest porcelain, love's tempest cannot win.

Harmony in Chaos

In the waltz of whispers, two souls entwine,
A dance of shadows, a shared design.
Folie à deux, a madness shared,
In love's deep ocean, fiercely bared.
Layer upon layer, their minds conflate,
With every heartbeat, they resonate.
A fusion so rare, a mirrored fate,
In each other's gaze, they find a mate.
Through stormy weathers and serene skies,
Their bond, a fortress that never dies.
In sync they laugh, in sync they weep,
In dreams, they soar, in love, they leap.
A duet of chaos, perfectly flawed,
Together they face a world abroad.
Folie à deux, their hearts decree,
In madness, they find their harmony.

Hamster Wheel

In the gallery of love, where hearts seek a muse,
Brushstrokes of passion, in reds and in blues.
A canvas of dreams, where we paint and erase,
Chasing the colors of an elusive embrace.
Round and round on the wheel of desire,
We run like hamsters, our spirits never tire.
With each turn, we hope for a change in the scene,
But the view stays the same—just a repetitive dream.
We mix our paints, with tears and with laughter,
Hoping this time, we'll find what we're after.
Yet the picture that forms, is one we know well,
A cycle of yearning, a hypnotic spell.
Insanity whispers, in strokes broad and fine,
"Love is a madness, both bitter and divine."
We dance to its rhythm, slaves to the beat,
In a waltz of devotion, both bitter and sweet.
So we spin in our circles, and paint once again,
On the canvas of love, where insanity reigns.
A masterpiece flawed, yet we can't help but crave,
The beautiful torment of love's endless wave.
Beneath the moon's pale watchful eye,
We cast our nets, again we try.
To capture stars within our grasp,
In love's relentless clasp.
Yet every star's a fleeting light,
A moment's joy, then out of sight.
And still we paint, with fervent zeal,

ECHO SHADE

On love's spinning wheel.
For in this dance of hope and fear,
We find the strength to hold what's dear.
And though we know it's quite insane,
We love, again and again.

Veil of Desire

Your presence lingers like a shadow's trace,
In the silence, I hear the echo of your grace.
The thought of you, a relentless chase,
A haunting melody I cannot erase.
In dreams, you dance, a fiery blaze,
In waking moments, a consuming phase.
A paradox of want, a perplexing maze,
In the labyrinth of you, forever I gaze.
Your essence, a potion I long to taste,
A sip of you, and reality is displaced.
In the tapestry of time, you're interlaced,
A forbidden fruit, in memory encased.
In the abyss of longing, I am faced,
With the ghost of your touch, I am graced.
A sweet torment, in my heart encased,
For you, I'd let all virtue be effaced.
In the quiet, I feel your unseen embrace,
A spectral caress, a yearning interface.
In the void, our souls would interlace,
In the dance of sin, our spirits chase.

Caution Tape

Approach me not with hopes of gleaming treasure,
For my heart's void, devoid of golden pleasure.
My spirit, a barren wasteland, not to trade,
A soul so lost, its worth cannot be weighed.
Seek warmth not in my frostbitten embrace,
Release your grip, my hand's a chilling space.
I am the winter, cold and uninviting,
A touch from me, stark as lightning striking.
Self-absorbed, I wander in my own shade,
Unmoved by the affections that you've laid.
Love's tender seed in me finds no ground to root,
Your care, unreturned, will wither to moot.
Draw near, and only pain shall you procure,
For I am flawed, my ways are impure.
You're a gem too precious for my coarse dirt,
Flee from my storm before you get hurt.
In this dance of shadows, I lead a lonesome waltz,
No symphony of love just echoes of my faults.
I'm a fortress of solitude, walls steep and sheer,
Where whispers of affection disappear.
Venture not into this labyrinth of despair,
Each corridor within echoes a silent prayer.
For the one who dares to enter, there's no guide,
Only memories of warmth that have long died.
I am the night, where stars refuse to shine,
A void so vast, where sun's rays never align.
Your light, though bright, cannot illuminate,

ECHO SHADE

The depths of my soul, forever desolate.

So, heed these words, a cautionary tale,

My presence is a ship destined to sail

Into the abyss, where love's light is snuffed,

Where hearts, once whole, leave broken and scuffed. Beware, for in my shadowed heart, love finds no berth,

A wanderer I remain, alone on this vast Earth.

Crescendo of Doubt

Gaze into my eyes,
Spin another web of lies,
Claim you'd meet demise,
Before you'd ever let me cry.
Swear your love is true,
Place no one else above, do you?
But the words feel worn, the sentiment askew,
Familiarity breeds contempt, and doubt accrues.
My name, once a sweet refrain,
Now lost, a forgotten melody in our domain,
Your actions altered, an unfamiliar strain,
Companionship constant, yet I feel the wane.
Explain this shift, this emotional exchange,
Your affection now feels estranged,
Absent I am, and your feelings rearrange,
No longer cherished, love deranged.
In solitude's wake, you profess to care,
When echoes of laughter no longer fill the air,
Once my luck, my charm so rare,
Now just a memory we barely share.
Persist in this charade, keep up the act,
But your love's not enough, it's an evident fact,
Time's ticking away, with each broken pact,
Soon my love will fade to black,
And from my eyes, no tears will track.

Calypso

In the shadowed alley of desire, she waits,
Her gaze, a woven spell of silken threads,
Luring the hearts of men to tempting fates,
With whispers soft as night, she gently treads.
She is Temptation, cloaked in midnight hues,
A siren song, the promise of forbidden fruit,
Her voice, the melody that souls seduce,
Leading astray with every tender flute.
Her touch, a fire, ignites the will to stray,
A dance of flames upon the edge of right,
Each step she takes, a path to lead away,
From virtue's day into indulgence's night.
She is the apple, sweet, the serpent's friend,
A lure to taste what's hidden, what's unseen,
In her embrace, the strongest wills may bend,
For she is queen where lesser queens have been.
Her eyes, a pool of deepest, darkest sin,
Reflecting back the yearnings deep within,
To dive into her depths, to swim and spin,
Is to accept the start of downfall's din.
She is the whisper in the moment's ear,
The choice that teeters on the edge of fall,
To follow her is to abandon fear,
And in her arms, to risk the loss of all.
Yet in her danger lies a strange allure,
A beauty in the risk, the chance, the play,
For those who seek the edges, less demure,

ECHO SHADE

She is the night that beckons to the day.
Temptation, she, a paradox of mind,
Both warning and the call to taste the thrill,
In her, the threads of destiny entwined,
The power to break, the power to fulfill.
So heed the call, or turn away, decide,
For she will be, no matter choice or time,
Temptation, ever present by our side,
A dance of danger, and a hint of sublime.

Casanova

In whispered tones they speak of him, a specter in the day,
A heartsmith forging love's deceit, as hearts he bends and sways.
A Bluebeard in a modern guise, with charm as his disguise,
He weaves a spell of sweet demise, beneath the lover's skies.
They say he'll read you like a book, with just a single glance,
A predator with roguish look, who leads you in a dance.
Once caught within his silken web, you'll never wish to flee,
But when he's gone, the thread will break, and so will part of thee.
Beware the man they call a thief, of hearts, of joy, of time,
For once he's had his fill of you, he'll leave you with a rhyme.
A ladies' man, they claim he is, a hunter in the night,
Who leaves a trail of broken dreams and vanishes from sight.
In the silence of his absence, echoes of whispers fill the air,
A haunting melody of memories, of a love that was so rare.
The aftermath is but a shadow, a hollow space where light once shone,
A garden where the roses withered, once he had roamed and gone.
The heart, once brimming with his presence, now feels the chill of loss,
A void where once there danced a flame, now covered in frost and moss.
The world spins on, indifferent, to the one he left behind,
A soul marooned in the wake of love, seeking what they cannot find.
Yet in this desolate landscape, where tears have watered ground,
New strength is found in solitude, and in the silence, sound.
For though the Casanova hunts, his prey becomes the wiser,
And from the pain of love's cruel game, a phoenix shall arise, sir.
As the night descends, another tale begins to weave,
A new heart lured by whispered promises, too naive.
In the moon's pale light, a silhouette, he casts his spell,

ECHO SHADE

Another soul to charm, ensnare, in love's ephemeral well.
Unseen, the threads of fate entwine, a pattern yet unseen,
The next in line, a heart unguarded, to the hunter's keen.
With every step, the dance continues, a rhythm set by time,
A cycle of enchantment, in this masquerade sublime.

Doom

Oh, the hilarity of heartache, where every 'I love you' feels like a comedic take.
Your sweet nothings were confections of deceit, honeyed words that were never meant to keep.
You played the angel, halo polished bright, but even Lucifer was once a creature of light.
Change was your promise, seen from afar, like spotting a pig flying to a star.
Love's sweetness turned tart, a dessert gone awry, where forever's promise was just a pie in the sky.
Time's funny that way, stretching and shrinking, an eternal bond now just weekend drinking.
The calm was a prelude, a deceptive peace, as warmth faded away like a summer's lease.
We left space for joy, a margin for error, not knowing it was room for impending terror.
We rolled out the red carpet, for love's grand parade, not seeing the potholes where our trust would degrade.
Cue the fanfare, the grand overture, for the guest of honor, disappointment so pure.
It arrived unannounced, without a hint of regret, a party crasher we'd rather forget.
But let's raise a glass to the end, my dear, and toast to the farce we held so near.
For in the theater of the absurd, our love played its part, a comedy of errors from the very start.
So here's to the punchline we never saw coming, to the jokes we lived, and the laughter now humming.
In the end, it's true, what they always say, 'Love is the ultimate comedy play.'

ECHO SHADE

And as the curtain falls, we take our bow, for the love that was, is just a chuckle now.

Aftermath

In the wake of our parting,
I rue the day's starting.
Facing life's stark reality,
Battling waves of anxiety.
Whispers urge a reckless cure,
A chilling thought I endure.
Fleeing to the hills for solace,
As sorrow's grip tightens its clasp.
Rouse me from this nightmare,
Where only fragments of hope dare.
My soul fractures with each scream,
Longing for the end of this dream.
Yearning for your presence at dawn,
For a message to lead me on.
Assurance that we'll be alright,
To endure the solitude of night.
Navigating the aftermath's maze,
Embarking on unfamiliar ways.
While I falter, seeking revival,
You've journeyed to a new arrival.
Our love story, once so bright,
A fairytale in the moonlight.
But your heart returned to the market,
My affection for you, now a closed docket.
Drowning sorrows in vintner's craft,
Embracing the glass, my makeshift raft.
It lacks a heartbeat, unlike mine,

ECHO SHADE

In this loveless void where I pine.
Still traversing the aftermath's course,
On a journey of recovery, I endorse.
My love for you was fervent and deep,
In every breath, a promise to keep.
Memories linger, hauntingly sweet,
Echoes of laughter, moments so fleet.
In the quiet, your shadow appears,
A dance of joy tinged with tears.
Each remembrance, a bittersweet refrain,
A melody of love, in loss, remains.
With each step, a new horizon unfolds,
A path of healing that the future holds.
Letting go of what was, embracing the now,
Moving forward, though I'm not sure how.
In every sunrise, I find a new pledge,
To cross the chasm, to leap from the ledge.

Chokehold

Many have come and gone, a fleeting parade,
Yet your memory lingers, in the silence it stayed.
I cherished you deeply, a treasure so rare,
A love like yours is beyond compare.
To numb the ache, I turn to the glass,
A temporary solace that soon will pass.
The morning's remorse, a familiar friend,
A cycle of sorrow, with no end.
Each kiss I steal, under the moon's soft gleam,
Lacks the magic of yours, a faded dream.
I extinguished our spark, a foolish game,
Now I'm haunted by the echo of your name.
I pushed you away, a reckless shove,
You offered me warmth, you offered love.
Now I'm reaping the cost, a lonely toll,
For steering my heart, away from its goal.
Nights stretch endless, a canvas of pain,
Tears carve rivers, an emotional strain.
My voice grows hoarse, as I call out your name,
In the silence, it's clear, I'm to blame.
Down the abyss, I lose my grip,
Despair's cold fingers, around my heart they slip.
Loneliness whispers, a chilling seep,
In its icy embrace, I'm lost in the deep.
Your hold on me, a ghostly chain,
A smile masks my heart's refrain.
But when spirits flow, my guard falls away,

ECHO SHADE

Words of anguish, I bitterly convey.
Absent you are, my cries just a stain,
In the void, my sorrow is lain.
Observers may watch, with a judging eye,
Unaware, it's your absence that makes me cry.
When the tequila's warmth spreads through my veins,
Memories flood back, sweet pleasure mixed with pains.
The tender moments we shared, now just a tease,
A haunting melody, carried on the breeze.
Your eternal grip, a bittersweet curse,
It drains my spirit and empties my purse.
A mental battle, a physical toll,
An emotional maelstrom, swallowing me whole.

Cry A River

In just a span of hours, our paths diverged,
A heart once whole, now splintered and scourged.
I tread alone, the pain fresh and stark,
Carrying the remnants of a love now dark.
Your pleas for me to stay, a desperate call,
Had me ensnared, believing in your thrall.
You claimed a love that was mine to claim,
Yet deceit was the heart of your game.
You fashioned faith where doubt should dwell,
A master of illusions, casting your spell.
But the truth unveiled your hollow creed,
And from your grasp, I am finally freed.
So let your tears fall, a deluge of sorrow,
For the love you mimicked but could not borrow.
Cry until the rivers rise and spill,
For I am gone, moved by stronger will.
The journey you face is one of your making,
A path of solitude, with no one partaking.
Through peaks of joy and valleys of woe,
You walk alone, reaping what you sow.
Promises of forever, a bond unbreakable,
Now revealed as nothing but fable.
You had me reaching for wallet and worth,
For vows empty of all their girth.
Your tears, a spectacle of feigned despair,
Claims of demise, an act laid bare.
Still, you weave lies, a tapestry so vile,

ECHO SHADE

In disbelief, I've watched for a while.
But no more shall I fall for your charade,
My belief in you, thoroughly betrayed.
I step forward, into a life anew,
Leaving behind the fiction that was you.
As the final curtain falls on our act so flawed,
I leave behind the facade you so artfully clawed.
In the quiet after the storm, I find my solace,
For in the end, it is my own peace I embrace.

December's Echo

Tonight, I steer through the dark,
To that old familiar landmark.
The neon lights a beacon to my shadow,
In this tavern, I find my shallow.
I've sought to erase,
To leave no trace,
Of memories in cold ember,
That night I can't dismember.
The silence of my heart's plea,
Echoes in the void you left in me.
In the mirror, a face of distress,
While you're out, chasing happiness.
To the bartender, I'm just another face,
Lost in the crowd, seeking solace.
In the clink of glass, a hollow cheer,
To the nights spent drowning fear.
You left me with dawn's ache,
For all the promises we break.
In the twilight's cruel jest,
I find no rest.
Was it something I didn't do,
That made you bid adieu.
For you, I'd brave the fray,
Yet here I am, led astray.
We were a tempest, wild and fierce,
Now just a tale, I sadly rehearse.
In the darkness, we were ablaze,

ECHO SHADE

Now I'm lost in this endless maze.
Again, I've sought to forget,
To let go of regret.
But your ghost lingers near,
In the December air, so clear.
You're the 6 a.m. thought,
In battles, I've fought.
The stranger's lips, a fleeting cure,
For a heart that's impure.
I scroll through our captured smiles,
A digital relic of forgotten miles.
It's all that's left, not gone,
In the silence of dawn.
You're the 6 a.m. sorrow,
The fear of tomorrow.
Time's a thief in the night,
Stealing you out of sight.
Still, I try to forget,
To forgive, not fret.
Yet, I can't help but remember,
That cruel bitter December.

Unsober October

The bartender and I, we're thick as thieves,
In the wake of your exit, I wear my heart on my sleeves.
The door shut behind you, and so I returned,
To the old haunts where my sorrows are burned.
No more pretense, the 'I'm fines' have run dry,
I've nothing left but the truth I deny.
It's been ages since we've met, my dear tequila,
You drown my woes, a potent panacea.
To the brim with grief, yet you ease the ache,
A temporary solace from the heartbreak.
Enter the scene, the infamous martini,
Stirred in memories, not shaken, uncanny.
Recalling wild nights, inhibitions cast aside,
Where I danced away the pain, nowhere to hide.

Silent Constellations

Beneath the veil of the night's embrace, he contemplates his solitude,
A heart once full, now a desolate state.
He gave her his all, but it was never enough,
Her love was a mirage, a bluff.
He walked through fire, for her, he'd brave the storm,
Yet in her eyes, he could never transform.
Into the knight, she dreamt in her sleep,
Leaving him in the abyss, so steep.
He whispered her name, a prayer in the dark,
Hoping she'd return and rekindle the spark.
But the silence was heavy, a suffocating shroud,
His voice, once bold, now barely loud.
He remembers her laughter, a haunting echo,
A melody that now sounds hollow.
She danced in the light, while he withered in the shade,
A cruel juxtaposition that fate had made.
He sought redemption in the preacher's wise words,
A solace for the pain that absurdly girds.
But the sanctuary he sought was a mirage in the sand,
His confessions lost, like whispers to the land.
He yearns for release from her spectral chains,
To find peace, where only her shadow remains.
But the memories linger, a relentless tide,
In the depths of his soul, where they reside.
He gazes at the stars, a celestial escape,
Wishing for a sign, a new shape.
But the heavens are silent, the constellations still,

ECHO SHADE

His plea for salvation, an unanswered will.
In the end, he knows, it's a battle within,
A war against a love that could never begin.
She was the dream he dared to chase,
A mirage of perfection, a destructive grace.
Now he stands alone, at the crossroads of his life,
Stripped of his passion, cut by strife.
The path ahead is uncertain, a journey blind,
But he must walk forward, leave her behind.
For in the end, it's the love for oneself that must suffice,
A lesson learned, a heavy price.
He'll rebuild his world, from the ashes of his heart,
A new beginning, a fresh start.

The Balm of Time

In the aftermath of love's casualty,
We reach for the first aid kit, hesitantly.
Bandages for trust, so carelessly torn,
Antiseptic for words, that were bitterly sworn.
Gauze wraps around memories, too painful to touch,
Tweezers pluck out shards of promises, once clutched.
Ointment soothes the burns of passion's fierce flame,
While ice packs cool the shame of playing love's game.
Each tool in the kit, a metaphor for time,
The healer of hearts, the rhythm and rhyme.
For just as flesh wounds mend and bones realign,
So too can the soul, with love's tender design.
We learn to forgive, not just others, but self,
To put past grievances back on the shelf.
To cleanse the wound, to start anew,
To give hope a chance, to see it through.
For in the end, it's not just about survival,
But about the journey, the heart's revival.
A first aid kit for the spirit, the mind,
A reminder that love, though lost, we can still find.
So let's restock our kits, not with fear or regret,
But with resilience, courage, and a willingness to bet.
On ourselves, on the future, on the unknown,
For the heart that's been broken, can still be sewn.
And just like the body's miraculous ability to heal,
Our capacity for love is just as real.
A broken relationship, a wound to the heart,

ECHO SHADE

Is but a moment in life, a chance to restart.
So here's to healing, to the power within,
To the first aid kit, and the strength to begin.
For every ending, a new beginning awaits,
And with it, a chance for love to reinstate.

The Lingering Question

When night falls, do you hear our laughter still?
Does it echo through your thoughts, against your present will?
Do the 'what ifs' and 'could haves' fill your mind's expanse,
Or are they just mere whispers, lost in time's vast dance?
Would you sift through memories, to find where we went wrong,
To unravel all the threads, in our love's once sweet song?
Would you dare to dream of us, a tapestry rewoven,
Or leave the past behind, its lessons duly proven?
Do you wander through the halls of what was never said,
Do the words hang in the air, or in your heart instead?
Do you ponder on the touch, the warmth that we once knew,
Or has time's relentless march, washed it away too?
Is there a space within your soul, where our story lies,
Or has it been archived, beneath life's newer skies?
Does the thought of 'us' ignite, a spark that softly glows,
Or is it just a shadow, of a rose that never grows?
In the silence of your world, do you ever pause and think,
Of the bond that we shared, now a missing link?
Does it haunt you like a melody, that sweet refrain,
Or is it buried deep, beneath the joy and pain?
For in the end, we're left with echoes of our tale,
A narrative of love, that either soars or fails.
And though we've walked our paths, now separate and apart,
The 'what ifs' keep on spinning, in the chambers of the heart.

Luci

Did it pain you when you fell,
From the celestial realms to a harsher spell?
Was dread your companion, relentless and dire,
As destiny's hand quenched your celestial fire?
Did sorrow's tear trace your ethereal face?
Once bathed in radiance, now shrouded in gloom,
Your halo, once brilliant, succumbed to doom.
A battle chosen, a war waged in vain,
Strength faltered, and victory remained arcane.
In the silence of night, do you find reprieve,
Or does restlessness turn, and tranquility leave?
Echoes of conflict, a relentless refrain,
Haunting visions of a throne you couldn't attain.
For power, for glory, a relentless quest,
To stand supreme, above the rest.
Engraved in eternity, your tale will persist,
A testament to the crown you almost kissed.
Now, a mere shadow, bereft of your prize,
A hound roaming, under tempestuous skies.
A visage marred by a scowl, a regal head unadorned,
The weight of a crown, from your brow scorned.
In disgrace, you bow, your legacy untold,
No prayers will rise for you, no temples of gold.
Fame, your cold comfort, a hollow embrace,
A life altered, never to regain its grace.
The prodigy once cherished, in a father's gaze,
Now a rebel cast out, lost in a labyrinthine maze.

ECHO SHADE

From cherished to renegade, a swift descent,
A trail of deception, of truths bent.
Ambition's fire kindled, a maelstrom unleashed,
In its wake, harmony ceased, and peace impeached.
A fall from grace, a plummet profound,
Hide your countenance, for shame abounds.

The Last Stanza

As the final page turns and the last verse settles, let us take a moment to reflect on the journey through the realms of rhythm and rhyme. We have traversed landscapes crafted from words, soared on the wings of imagination, and delved into the depths of emotion. May the echoes of the verses resonate within, stirring the soul long after the book is closed. And in the quiet that follows, may you find the inspiration to pen your own path, for every end is but a promise of a new beginning. Thank you for sharing this poetic adventure.

Don't miss out!

Visit the website below and you can sign up to receive emails whenever ECHO SHADE publishes a new book. There's no charge and no obligation.

https://books2read.com/r/B-A-HQCXB-YNAUD

BOOKS 2 READ

Connecting independent readers to independent writers.

About the Author

Echo Shade, a name that whispers of mystery and creativity, marks the literary debut of an author whose passion for the written word has culminated in their first published work. This enigmatic writer, choosing to step into the literary world under a veil of anonymity, brings a fresh voice to the realm of storytelling. With a deep appreciation for the classics of literature, Echo Shade has long been an ardent admirer of the power of stories to transport readers to other worlds, times, and experiences. This reverence for the art form sparked a desire to contribute their own threads to the rich tapestry of literary tradition.

The journey to authorship was born from a wellspring of inspiration drawn from the vast ocean of literary masterpieces. Echo Shade's inaugural book is not just a labor of love, but a bold step into the arena of imagination and narrative. It represents a bridge between the timeless allure of storytelling and the personal creative vision that has been nurtured over years of reading and reflection.

Beyond the fictional landscapes, Echo Shade harbors a keen interest in the realms of non-fiction, with a particular penchant for the intricate and often macabre details of true crime, as well as the sweeping narratives of history. These subjects, rich with complexity and humanity, are the next frontier that Echo Shade aims to explore in their upcoming projects. The author is currently delving into research, seeking to uncover truths and weave them into compelling accounts that will captivate readers who share a fascination for the real stories that shape our world.

As Echo Shade embarks on this literary voyage, they stand at the confluence of past influences and future aspirations. Their work is a testament to the enduring beauty of literature and its capacity to enlighten, challenge, and entertain. With a foot in the storied past and an eye on the horizon of future works, Echo Shade is poised to make a lasting impression on the literary landscape, inviting readers to join them on a journey of discovery and wonder. Echo Shade's narrative is just beginning, and the pages ahead promise to be filled with the intrigue and insight that only a true devotee of literature and life's truths can provide.

9 7 9 8 2 2 7 1 4 0 1 2 8